MW01388923

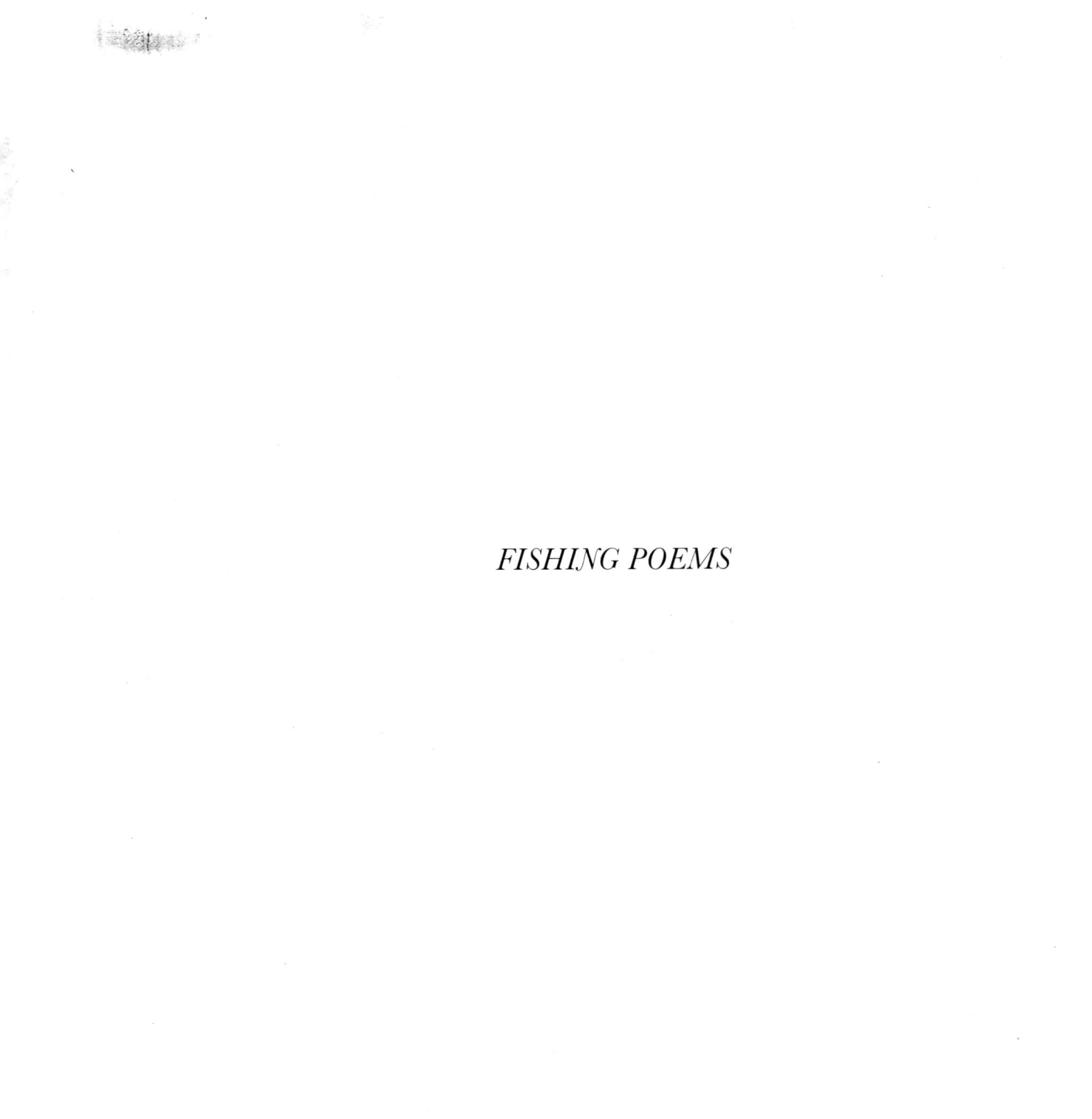

FISHING POEMS

FISHING POEMS
Karen Mulhallen

Black Moss Press
EST. 1969

2014

© 2014 Karen Mulhallen

Library and Archives Canada Cataloguing in Publication

Mulhallen, Karen, author
    Fishing poems / Karen Mulhallen.

ISBN 978-0-88753-539-0 (pbk.)

    I. Title.

PS8576.U414F58 2014   C811'.54   C2014-903740-6

Designer: Brad Smith.

Black Moss Press
EST. 1969

Published by Black Moss Press at 2450 Byng Road, Windsor Ontario, Canada, N8W 3E8.
Black Moss books are distributed in Canada and the U.S. by Fitzhenry & Whiteside. All orders should be directed there.

Black Moss Press acknowledges the support of the Canada Council for the Arts and the Ontario Arts Council for its publishing program.

ONTARIO ARTS COUNCIL
CONSEIL DES ARTS DE L'ONTARIO

Canada Council for the Arts   **Conseil des Arts du Canada**

PRINTED IN CANADA

Earth, Water, Air, Fire

This book is dedicated to Ontario's heartland, the deep southwest,
and to all those who find their well-springs there

CONTENTS

I: *The Fishing Poems, An Album* 9

II: *Ondine's Lament* 17

III: *The Sailor's Letter* 21

IV: *The Village* 39

- *The Early Settlement* 40
- *Children at the Beach* 60

V: *The Narrative of John Simple* 71

VI: *Arrivals* 85

Afterword and Acknowlegements 88

Time is but the stream I go a-fishing in. I drink at it, but while I drink I see the sandy bottom and detect how shallow it is. Its thin current slides away, but eternity remains.

Henry David Thoreau, *Walden* (1845)

I
THE FISHING POEMS, AN ALBUM

I have kept my *Fishing Poems* close by for many decades. Their essential topography began to develop in my childhood and adolescence. As a family, we often drove from Woodstock in my father's bright red Buick on hot summer weekends to Lake Erie to the Houghton Sand Hills, or we constructed a picnic in the parks and the beaches at Long Point, Turkey Point and Port Dover. Sometimes my parents would rent a cottage, a small wooden shack.

In adolescence, when the freedom offered by the family car came into play, I went with other teenagers to hear music: Rompin' Ronnie Hawkins, Alice Cooper, Chuck Berry; they all performed in Ontario's deep southwest.

And more rarely, but memorably, in adulthood, my brothers and I would go off to spend the day in west Norfolk at the Houghton Sand Hills, towering 250 feet in the air, ever changing, and shaped toward the east by the southwest winds which revealed potshards and arrowheads in their passage and the shadowy presence still of a look-out,

9

aboriginal or white, gauging the approach of a stranger across the long narrow stretch of lake below. *Erielhonan*, Iroquois for long-tailed.

Welded with these scenes was my indelible reading, when I was thirteen, of Alain Bombard's *Naufragé Volontaire* (1953). Bombard sailed across the Atlantic from France to the Barbados, a distance of 4400 km, in an open boat, an inflatable he invented himself, and which he called *L'Hérétique*. With only a sextant, a few provisions, and an indomitable will, Bombard epitomized for me all those other great voyages on the oceans of the world, all those heretical abandonments of the known, those searches for a new found land.

It is easy to get shipwrecked, or to drown, in the search for freedom.

*

In the early seventies, I lived in Toronto in a second floor apartment in a house on Brunswick Avenue. In the rear ground floor apartment was a photographer named Brian Ramer who hailed from Brantford. It was Brian who initiated my tertiary enchantment with Norfolk County as we explored our shared childhoods and talked of climbing the towering Houghton Sand Hills, white grains slithering between fingers and toes, and the shallow warm welcoming waters and sun-dappled sandy beach at Port Dover on the shores of Lake Erie.

Brian was making a living as a photographer and spending all his spare time in our back yard teaching himself solarized printing. The old buildings of Spadina Avenue with their cross hatchings of street car lines, their eccentric turrets and false façade pediments and elaborate brickwork niches would appear in brown and the palest gold, like ancient sepia prints, on sheets of paper, spread over the weeds under the clothesline. Upstairs, I'd given up Near Eastern Studies and Archaeology and was teaching myself structural linguistic analysis with an eye on those lush passionate melancholic tales of William Faulkner.

Four of us piled in Brian's old chevie and drove off for the day to Dover. Brian had been a couple times lately, talked to John Simple, and hung out on the beach, eating foot-long Arbors and watching the farm kids from Hagersville with their six foot inflatables, the big kings of the surf.

It was a tiny town, not much bigger than in Brébeuf's time, although now it was all white. Brian had walked the main drag. Mr Vary still had his store at #421 Main street which he'd set up in 1908, when there were 1500 folks in the town. It took nearly forty years to double that. He was 87 now, but his memory was good, which is what we found in everyone we talked to.

We headed up St Andrew which curves like a comma back to Main at the Water Tower. It was early, the beach mottled from the night rain, the sun rays small. For a moment it clouded over, and the sun shone through an aperture, the narrow band a hot vertical arc light. The tide was coming in, the water flashing diamonds in front of a large white yacht. A small blue sailboat cut across the bay, just behind a coral yacht at anchor. I knew by noon the whole beach would be a quilt, one blanket after another. The Blue Pickerel was still the best fish shack on the beach, "no bones about it," but at that hour we had no inclination to "Try some for the Halibut," despite the faded old sign, hung proudly on its front. And anyway the louvres were only partly open.

The gulls were swooping around a fishing boat way out there. We squinted into the sun as a yellow paper bag came floating along the horizon line, like a double-masted iceberg. Then we decided to climb up toward the drawbridge through the underbrush, dead twigs snap snapping against dusty gravel. Just then the bells began to ring.

My sandals were no good for climbing and I had to pick my way barefoot around fallen thistle burrs, old nails, and cigarette butts. The bridge began to lift, cutting a diagonal right across the sky, as a bird with a fish by the tail came swooping under, heading up the canal toward the river. There were three kids on the bridge, a couple of bikes dumped by the side on the gravel slope. Two of the kids had fishing poles, and there was a large tomato juice can full of minnows on the ground.

We were going to talk to John Simple in the evening, about gill netting in an open boat and about dragging for smelt, and the lore of the town. We knew where the Alma would dock and I'd already put my hand down into the split car-tire buoys full of small soft spiders lining the Alma's spot.

Brian and Tony climbed up to the top of Bank street on the edge of the highway, just over from the big yellow fork-lift machine, while Bill and I went on another amble in the town centre. We knew we'd all end up back on the beach to make a supper out of golden orange sweet Honey Glow drinks, a dog and an ice cream cone at the Arbor shack, where a scoop of blueberry or loganberry was only 10 cents.

Near the dock was a mass of orange net and a pile of green and white and grey buoys. The Dover Rose slid into harbour loaded down. We picked up the boardwalk and headed to Globe & Mail Park where we all met up with Shelley and Sheri and Dougie playing on the stone lions at the bandstand steps. I figured them for 13 or so, and I wasn't far off. We did the standard adult tack, asked them about school. "You guys are lucky. I don't learn nothin in school," said Dougie. "The other kids are too noisy." "Is the teacher young?" "No, but not old either. She's got veins in her hands." Brian's camera was handed over and Sheri cracked a real Marilyn Monro cheesecake. "She looks sharp without the camera," says Dougie, "through it she doesn't even look smart."

Brian and I went several more times to Dover that summer to walk the beach, to talk to the fishermen, and to spend time in the small town library archives.

*

When I was growing up in southwestern Ontario, the past and its passions were everywhere present. I went to the Indian reserve at Ohsweken with my father, and to farm auctions where old farm houses and barns yielded vestiges of pioneer days. In July, there were Highland Games nearby at Embro, and the Battle of Culloden was fought over and over, as children in kilts danced over swords, and the Amish families, all modestly dressed, arrived with their horses and buggies. The world champion tug-of-war team, originating in the 1870s, was a group of six farmers who lived near Embro. They called themselves *The Mighty Men of Zorra*, after the township they lived in. For a child there was always an odd sense that many of the rituals I encountered and the people I met had come from away. How did they get here; what was this place for them; were they really here, or were they still there?

And always beyond the early settlers and their descendants and the native peoples there loomed the distant past, a world of animal and spirit forms, manifesting themselves in nature.

*

While I lived on Brunswick Avenue, Lorraine Monk had published, for the National Film Board of Canada, a book to celebrate Canada's centenary, a picture book, *Canada: A Year of the Land*, with poems by my friend Miriam Waddington. Brian Ramer and I were inspired by its format and began to plan our own book of text and pictures. When our book was done, I sent it to the NFB and then to two other publishers, and it has remained unpublished. Brian left 411 Brunswick and eventually I moved on as well. But before I left Brunswick Avenue I went to the Pacific Ocean where I met a sailor who had built his own trimaran and sailed south from northern California, past the Baja coast where the spirits and the winds are strong, to a small fishing village on the west coast of Mexico.

I can still hear the crackle of the light blue onionskin airmail letters as they slipped through the front door mail slot bearing the beginnings of yet another version of *Fishing Poems*. For although my fishing poems had begun in childhood, they also now included the death, by drowning in the Tiber, of my friend Chris, as well as the end of my marriage, which had been primarily enacted by water, to a man who had been schooled on a ship, as his own father was its commander. So although I was born landlocked, I was early, or from the very beginning, marked by water.

I met the sailor on the beach in the old fishing village of Zihuatenejo. I had been to a shack for dinner, where a thin, grey-haired white woman in pajamas, hands shaking, served us dishes of lobster by the light of an oil lamp hung on a peg from the roof rafters. Afterward L and I went for a walk on the beach, and then took a taxi up the hill to our hotel, The Irma, determined to move to the beach in the morning. B was on the beach that night, but I didn't know it.

The next morning, settled in to our beachfront double room, with its louvres opening toward the sea, we took a stroll and met the crew of the Tattoo, three tall bleached-out northern California sailors, of which B was the captain.

Ixtapa was being carved out of the cliffs, south of town, and we ran along the coast in the Tattoo looking up at tiny figures crawling like white ants over the face of the rocks. We beached below the vast hive, ate shrimp cooked on an open fire by a local fisherman, then walked up to the waterfalls, and stood under the cascades, fully clothed, as the water plastered hair, dresses, shorts, and T-shirts to bodies.

The following day, just before noon, we went up the hill to the village lending library, where I showed B the diaries of Simone Weil, while the resident king parrot squawked, and then took a bite out of my finger.

In the morning, L and I took a light plane back to Mexico City. I can still remember looking out from the small porthole down on the rough field landing strip where B stood tall against the wooden shacks, his long blond ponytail still damp from our morning shower.

It would be more than twenty years before I let myself fall in love again with a sailor, and in the meantime I would have taken to the sea myself.

*

The *Fishing Poems* and the deep southwest have stayed with me and I have carried my manuscript to Scotland, to Venice, to Australia and to Toronto Island. Anyplace I went on retreat to write, the *Fishing Poems* went with me, always rewritten, never released. They have allowed me to write about the Caribbean Sea, the Atlantic Ocean, the Baja Peninsula, the Great Barrier Reef, and that great fresh water sea at the base of the city which is my home, Lake Ontario.

I have come to recognize that my relationship with the *Fishing Poems* and with water is a trope writers know intimately. There is a book always close to you that you cannot finish and cannot truly let go. It is the catalyst for other excursions. If you are William Faulkner, it is your Golden Book of Yoknapatawpha County; if you are Mavis Gallant, it is your study of the Dreyfus Case; if you are Mr Casaubon, in George Eliot's *Middlemarch*, it is your very *Key to All Mythologies*. Fictional authors or the real McCoy, there is always the book which eludes and leads us.

II
ONDINE'S LAMENT

I have been acquainted with absence;
Neither air nor water is my element.
I have been acquainted with absence,
Moving as amphibious creatures ought.

The old woman warned me
Returning from the arroyo:
You have remained out too long, she said,
After dark is dangerous.

I am the air when full—
My heart is beating;
I am the evening wind—
My blood is coursing.

Here the wings of the fragrant fly
Mimic my flight,
Holding me in his embrace
Clasping my clasping hands.

When it is damp, the water sinks—
My eyes are flickering.
When it is dry, the fountain sprays—
My veins are pulsing;

When it is sunning, the prisms crack—
My core is throbbing.
When it is darkling, the stars shine—
Myself am waiting:

Neither fish nor fowl
Always smooth but plumed:
Myself am waiting,
Myself am curling,

Myself am turning
Toward the horizon without end,
Shore without line, sound without presence:
The voice, the touch, the texture,
       which renews.
I am not Griselda, nor was meant to be,
  am an attendant slave

…we ourselves see in all rivers and oceans. It is the image of the ungraspable phantom of life; and this is the key to it all.
Herman Melville, *Moby Dick*, 'Loomings' (1851)

III
THE SAILOR'S LETTER

1.

Time to Leave

Mother came to me and the moon was full. The boat rocks gently around me making quiet gurgling noises, in the soft warm breeze. An ancient shadow moves through me. My hair is damp from swimming in the phosphorescent water. The moon's energy is palpable.

Daily the clouds tower higher above the hills—cumulus stacking up ten thousand feet—and after the evening spectacle, after the quiet holy hour before darkness, the thunder rolls through. It's time to leave. Cyclones threaten and the coast is dangerous.

Today we took some sun sights with the sextant, working out our position, giving us more confidence in the mystery of celestial navigation. As I write, I am looking at your picture, your face in shadow, a face kissed on the beach. Two white birds flew into the dawn sky.

The part of me you keep, keep it warm, as the part of you that lives here makes me gentle.

2.

It's a warm windless evening at least 1580 nautical miles from anything you can walk on. This is our second night of calm. The sails came down just after I went on watch at midnight. Then we all slept and I had a vivid dream in which you were with me, your face clear at last. In all my pictures, your face is wreathed in dark wind-blown hair, silhouetted against the setting sun.

It doesn't feel like we're so far from land as we are, and the nights in calms are just like being at anchor, although there is a great stillness. Much time for reflection.

3.

Nine days later, evening, becalmed,

In the waiting there are many dreams—the half moon behind the ragged clouds, the soft sparkle of phosphorescent animals, as the boat slightly rocks in what remains of the swell. Lamp-lit cabins, and companions so close we need hardly speak.

4.

Two days on

Often lately I have had a feeling, almost a déjà vu of childhood—but that's not quite it. It's warm and bright like a jar of honey in the sun, sweet and beatific; in it I care for nothing.

Just went on deck, for the motion of the boat has changed—moon-lit sky, moon-lit sea, moon-lit the bright sails. The wind has increased, and we're making seven and a half knots in the power of these two great forces, the wind and the sea.

5.

Nightfall

We're flying down the seaway before a fair wind at six knots, with a gentle rocking surging motion, as each sea overtakes us from the stern, lifting, so that the boat rushes down it, before the sea passes underneath, and the next lifts us again.

We sailed this way all last night and I dreamt a beautiful dream that I had delivered a baby.

The sky was grey almost all day until sunset when the cloud cover broke. The cloud and sky covers here are unlike anything I've ever seen. Not more spectacular, but the colours are somehow different. It is the sky that holds me, on a vertiginous swing between the known and the other, like finding a stranger in your home as you enter.

6.

<u>water</u>
One thinks always of the water supply, waiting, waiting for the wind.

<u>dolphin</u>
The past few days there have been many dolphins following the boat
for hours at a time. Three days ago about twenty came to us in the morning
just as we were finishing breakfast, and they stayed for hours, swimming easily in front
of the bows, rising and blowing, flashing in the sparkling water.

In the bright morning sun, they led us like the horses of charioteers.
They make me ecstatic when they come around. Talking in high-pitched squeaking
among themselves, one to another.
   Something ancient, antique, forgotten.

7.

Evening

We're rushing on through the moonlit night with land some 1800 nautical miles dead over the bows.

We've been running fast and smooth all day, before a 16 knot wind in a five foot seaway and we made 154 miles in 24 hours.

I took two sun sights with the sextant, four hours apart, and I got a good fix of our position. Navigation on the open sea, the old friendship with the sun.

8.

Rain

Heavy rain just at dawn. The first we've had. It was cold and coming down hard, but it felt good on my naked body.

I unlashed and turned the dinghy right side up, while I held a big yellow mixing bowl under the gooseneck (where the boat joins the mast). My bowl was filled over and over and emptied into five gallon cans. We bailed the dinghy with a soup bowl and captured about eight gallons, which really takes the squeeze off the water supply.

Soon the sun was shining, and the three of us, naked as is our custom, were back at our usual daily occupations: watching the sky and sea, doing little maintenance jobs, and navigating. And so our day passed.

9.

Our life at sea has been quite peaceful, yet always we know that sooner or later heavy weather must come.
    A clear night, and we lay together on deck, looking up at the moons of Jupiter, trying to recall all their names.

10.

<u>Seven more days</u>

Full moon and our spirits are light and bright as the dancing sea. We've had three wonderfully exhilarating days of fast sailing in perfect conditions, logging 154, 166 & 176 nautical miles.

The little crosses on our chart are marching towards land in long steps.

11.

<u>Land birds</u>

Our lives here are simple, cyclical, rhythmic, woven into the phases of the moon and the weather.

Today land birds visited the boat twice.

The moon is full, its shadows are sharp, and the boisterous sea gleams. A flying fish just came on deck. Natural selection operates; the silly ones get eaten.

12.

We've been boiling along with a great rooster tail wake, with the setting sun dead over the bows.

About half an hour ago, the big red-orange full moon began to rise behind us on the horizon, breaking in and out of the clouds, yellowing as it rose.

Now, as I sit in the aft cabin, writing by lamplight, it's a silver sphere shining in the back window.

13.

<u>The dog watch, 2:00 a.m.</u>

Moon lit, warm, and clear, no rain squalls yet.
I'm alone here with a harness around my chest and shoulders.
There's enough line to give me the freedom of the deck on a night like this.
I can go below or wander about, sitting perhaps on the quarter deck behind the cabin, watching the wake stream out behind, as night moves toward morning.

Tonight there'll be no echoing shouts, as an indifferent boat disappears into the dark.

14.

Summer Solstice

Rushing, thumping sea, an inky darkness and the masts are threatening to come down. The headsail sheets are whipping all about the deck.

All day the skies and sea were leaden, and the trades blew and blew.
Like a runner at the tape, like a horse at the gate, all day she strained, then slithered down the mounting seas.

One sea, larger and steeper than the rest, lifted her stern high and sent her into a magnificent, heart-stopping sleigh ride which went on and on. Suddenly we were sideways and then backwards, with the sails drawing back.

Cacophony of wind and sea and our voices shouting into the gale.

Now she's moving like an express train without a star to guide her and even the usually phosphorescent wake is dim in the yellow gleam of the cabin lamps.

15.

Four days later
June 29, Afternoon

The sea approached must have an affect on the spirit.
Crossing this ocean, we have lived in seclusion, in a state of blissful anarchy,
with only nature as our guide.

Night came so very softly to us, the sky all over dusky rose, the sea mauve;
away on the horizon that pale robin's egg blue that leads you out
to where the secrets are.

For I am making to the shore day by day, the Lord Jesus take me.
Christopher Smart, *Jubilate Agno* (1759-63)

16.

I July—a hot afternoon

LAND HO! Just went on deck and there it is. Heavy, grey-black on the horizon under the clouds, right over the bows, and on schedule.

The hills so green. The land lush-looking and beautiful as we glide the last few miles up the coast into a bay, on the last whispers of a failing wind, just at sunset.

Our anchor down at last, after 25 days at sea, almost all our food gone. We rowed ashore and took a little walk around. Walking was strange and good.

It's all a montage now, Sarah. Looking back on it—two white birds in a windy sky.

17.

LAND HO! Just went on deck, and there it is.
Heavy, grey-black, on the horizon under the clouds,
right over the bows, and on schedule.

Ah Sarah, the hills are so green. The land lush and beautiful
as we glide the last few miles up on the last whispers
of a failing wind at sunset.

IV
THE VILLAGE

Does not the worm erect a pillar in the mouldering church yard?
And a palace of eternity in the jaws of the hungry grave

William Blake, *Visions of the Daughters of Albion* (1793)

THE EARLY SETTLEMENT,
Lynmouth and Dover

1.

May 15, 1814. Afternoon, 3 p.m.

May my words revive this village, its old time glories;
May my words rescue its past from the day
we soldiers crowded the schooner's deck,

suddenly loomed from the fog-covered lake,
haunted by rattlesnakes and sea monsters,
we came like Mishepeshu:

Eight hundred strong we camped, just past Globe & Mail park,
east of the little creek flowing through Dover:

From our landing, the village was a mere mile;
From our landing, the village was next morning gone.

2.

This place is a point on a journey; no maps survive:
the traveler arrives at a territory of painted cougars, mountain lions,
snakes, deer, bustards, elk, and beaver,
turkeys, cranes and bitterns.

The settlement grows, thriving, ancient village
starts from a black root in the meadow,
passes the basswood stump on the river bank,
extends to a marked tree in the sugar camp,

ends at that lovely, treacherous sheet of water.

3.

Characters present themselves as eccentrics:
All an unusual cargo.
Our Prime Minister, for example, bibulous Sir John A. Macdonald
leans over to his colleague, H. C. Becker, urges him on:
"More power to your elbow."
And there's Robert Nichol, builder of grist and saw mills—
A man who would not be cowed.

4.

The press is here too from the beginning:
The Fourth Estate of the Realm,
The Dover Argus sketches the contours of community:
inns, industry, landscape, law, shipping, ship building—

The Houghton Arms, The Old Poplar Inn, The Village of Lynn, The Steamboat Hotel, The Houghton Ironworks, Rattlesnake Harbour, Lake Hunger, Brandy Creek, Died With Their Boots On, The Houghton Sand Hills, The Dog's Nest Tavern, The Halfway House, Marr's Hollow, Doan's Hollow, and that palatial steamer Kaloolah.

Names, each redolent with history, human events, stories.

4b.

Interlude by James Fenimore Cooper, from *The Prairie* (1827)

"...a gull would have to fan a thousand miles of air to find the eastern sea. And yet it is no mighty reach to hunt across, when shade and game are plenty. The time has been when I followed the deer in the mountains of the Delaware and the Hudson, and took the beaver on the streams of the upper lakes, in the same season; but my eye was quick and certain at that day, and my limbs were like the legs of a moose. The dam of Hector was then a pup, and apt to open on the game the moment she struck the scent. She gave me a deal of trouble, that slut, she did!"

5.

An Unusual Cargo

Gulls gather, rise screaming, circling, dipping, but the pier is idle;
occasionally a small sailboat glides by.

Now and then a fishing tug stirs the waters, casting refuse catch overboard.

Then the barge Thomas Ivey steals in, discharging its cargo of coal.

It is a June day, in the year of our Lord, 1856, the 28th day of that month,
or so it was recorded by Captain Fuller, immigration agent.
Busiest harbour on the north shore, today oddly silent.

Two rakish masts appear, square sail at foretop,
long laden jib-boom. Speculations commence and Captain Fuller, loathe to join in,
wrinkles his brow.

Deepest yearnings join the fray, Gunny Walker is waiting for gun barrels; for Sam
Garner, a sculptor of more than ordinary skill, slabs of marble. Others crave tea, coffee,
snuff.

The bark Nonsuch sails in as a righteous old salt remarks she surely is an Atlantic coast
trader.

Some think she carries the bell for St Paul's newly erected—
a sturdy bell to summon the tardy to service, guide ships through fog to harbour.

A barrel of crackers and a keg of oysters for Dan Drake; medicines for Dr Crouse; tea,
coffee, tobacco, snuff for Scovil & Scofield.

Scythes, potatoes and forks for I.W. Powell & Son; bundles of hide for Lawson and Bennett.

And drugs for R.M. Stephens, first druggist, adding to his custom, tortuously extracting teeth with a primitive turnkey.

The registers of the customs house lie open, recounting other tales of yearning, molasses and moscovado sugar, hoops for barrels and crinolines and children, nuts, candies and tart oranges for the Christmas trade.

Captain Fuller dips his quill in the inkwell, as the Captain of the Nonsuch enters the elegant customs house, log in arms. Villagers press their noses against the windows.

Captain Fuller pauses a moment, looks at the log, looks at the door, looks at the windows, and begins to enter:

39 Oirish Colleens and as fine a lot as ever come from the owld sod, come to make a new breed, Irish, Scots, English and Indian.

5b.

June 28, 1856
The bark Nonsuch landed;
Immigration officer Captain Fuller records:
Question:
What cargo have you?
Reply:
39 emigrant girls and baggage

"Thorty-noine Oirish colleens Sor" was the reply, *"and as foine a lot as ever come from the owld sod. But may the divel fly away wit' me if ever i ship sich a cargo ag'in. Will behaved, they were, and moighty polie, but begorrah, they were under fut everywhere, till the only place a seaman could found elbow-room was aloft in the riggin. Sure, the crew could hardly kape at their worruk fur starin' at them."*

6.

July 18, 1834
William Pope's Journal

Daylight appeared and found some were yawning,
some were stretching, and some were fast asleep.

7.

Captain Alexander McNeilledge
(1791-1874)

Captain Alexander McNeilledge committed suicide at the age of 83.
This is the last entry in his diary, 20 August 1874:

*I last saw my mother on July 12, 1806, when I left Scotland expecting to be gone 3 or 4 months.
I was shipwrecked, and did not return to Scotland for 40 years.*

They were all shipwrecks, maddened, these men,
gathered in that village in the wood, dreaming of prosperous towns,
perchance a great city, other civilizations,
the bonnie, bonnie banks o' Loch Lomond.

One log house, the Birdsells, halfway to Van Allen's place;
a small house on Prospect Hill, where Silas Knight the lawyer lived.
A school was raised; and at the mill, a small store,
kept by John Kirkpatrick and Colin McNeilledge—

And that mill, *The Granary*, haunted by Rob Roy, on its fascia mounted
the figurehead of the schooner called *Highlander*
wrecked on the treacherous sheet of water,
painted in Campbell and MacGregor colours,

and each 30th of November, St Andrew's night,
Scots gather at Sandy's Tavern in Dover,
raising a glass, drinking a dram, crying aloud
with haggis and pipes, and all the accompaniments,

skirling their longing,
Red Robert, Red Robert,
Rob Roy, Rob Roy

8.

Attiwandarouk,
Poem for the Neutrals

Bred of Algonquins, early settlers found
a people called Neutrals, a people pacific,
Nation Neutre, Attiwandarouk;
the Hurons said their language was awry.

And I saw them quite early one morning at planting
sunflowers, pumpkins, beans, tobacco,
corn and squash. Naked, they were so alive.

One told me he came in the fourteenth century,
many winters he called it, when the land still
abounded in deer, elk and beaver,

bustards and cranes, turkeys and bitterns,
squirrels and painted cougars.
Our early school reader called them
The Cats.

And in those first years, they went naked in the sun,
donned skins in winter, baked with earthen pots,
wove rush mats, stalked fish and deer.
Who were these Neutrals, painted with ochre,
red berries, white clay, and soot?

Who were these Cat people, these farmers,
their hair grotesque and startling:
loose on one side, tightly braided on the other,
or worse yet, quite shaven, save one long lock,
or a ridge across the crown?

Who were these people, madly decorated,
faces and bodies frequently tattooed,
painted with ochre, white clay, soot, and red berries?

Theirs the first village at Dover.
4000 warriors Champlain counted,
but not their women or their mules.

Their dead they kept by them in their dwellings,
falling flesh hung from trees and scaffolds,
intolerable the smell.

Their Feast of the Dead, periodic mass burials,
interring Aegyptian-style, pots and utensils,
weapons, and ornaments, bodies and bones.

1616, the year of Champlain's visit;
1640, Brébeuf's mission found only 3000 there.
Today, ossuaries, hidden, in a remote compound.

9.

The ancient village of Dover was once high above the lake where three roads made a small triangle. The first two streets were Maiden Lane and Queen street and joining the Gravel road they ran down a little hill, across an old bridge, past a ruined mill and curled up to Prospect Hill. After the village was burned, rebuilding was slow and moved south to the lake to become Port Dover. In 1835 Maiden Lane became Main street, leading to the river, parts of it still remain.

10.

Blue Pickerel, best fish in town /
No bones about it.

11.

Deacon Kitchen's story might be a poem, about faith and revelation, the power to move if not mountains at least men.

According to legend, Kitchen was a wild young Newton, New Jersey, man, converted by Dover's Richard Lanning. After his awakening, Kitchen walked 500 miles through the wilderness of Upper Canada, bearing witness, heading for Lanning.

On his back was a knapsack, in front of him was the Hudson River. He followed it up to Albany, west to Rochester, and along the shore to Turkey Point.
50 miles a day, knapsack for a pillow; by night he warded off the wolves.

No darkness to light, this conversion. No sudden blue bolt. Lanning's greeting shattered his faith,
"What, why Jo, you don't know anything about religion. True conversion is just like popping out of the tar barrel into the blazing light of the noonday sun."

12.

A Diary

1793 Peter Walker, first settler, builds a log cabin at the mouth of the Lynn
1793 William Frances petitions Simcoe for a grant
1801 Daniel McQueen, son of Alexander, builds the first mill
1813 Battle of Lake Erie, Captain Barclay defeated, but not disgraced
1814 May 15, The beautiful village on which the sun shone in splendour that morning, before 2 p.m. a heap of smoldering ruins. After the burning, the land lay untenanted, villagers move away, most lots sold
1816 Death of Henry Bostick, Norfolk's popular first lawyer

Beginning again:

1828 A new mill
1830 A school
1831 First Post Office
1833 Steamboat Hotel
1835 Israel Woods Powell lays out the new village of Port Dover
1843 The year of the plank and gravel road
1950 March, Fishing tug, *Anjoe K* sunk in Port Dover Harbour
1953 August, Treasure sighted on the bottom of Lake Erie, but never found
1954 Waterworks begun
1957 Three boats caught fishing in American waters. First trawler used out of Dover
1960 New pier constructed. Dover's fleet becomes the largest fresh water fishing fleet in the world
Rompin' Ronnie Hawkins plays on the pier. Frog legs served at the attendant buffet

1970 Three hotels, seven service stations, Still one of the world's largest fishing fleets. One public school, one high school, and many "historical" sights
1971 Sunday, September 5, 2 p.m. until midnight, Chuck Berry plays at the Summer Garden; Friday, September 17, 7 p.m. Alice Cooper plays in Hamilton at the Brian Timmins Stadium

13.

HEADLINES FROM THE LOCAL NEWSPAPER

MIKE TROYER'S CANOE LADEN WITH WILD TURKEYS

NORFOLK'S FIRST WHITE MAN, BILLY SMITH, FALLS DOWN

PIONEER ODDS AND ENDS

TRIED BY GOD AND THEIR COUNTRY AT TURKEY POINT

BOXED UP BY HIS WIFE, ABRAHAM SMITH

PIONEER CHICKENS HATCHED IN TRANSIT

WHISKEY, A MEDIUM OF EXCHANGE

TWO BROTHERS MEET IN DEADLY COMBAT AT LUNDY'S LANE

A PIONEER MOTHER WHO WEIGHED 300 POUNDS

OUR GRANDFATHERS STRUGGLE WITH THE FOREST

FIRST WHITE BURIAL IN OLD CHARLOTTEVILLE—FREDERICK MABEE

TITUS FINCH OLD SOLDIER PREACHER

THE OLD WOODHOUSE SQUIRE WHO KISSED THE BRIDE

WALKED 500 MILES TO TELL HIS FRIEND HE WAS CONVERTED

WONDERFUL PEDESTRIAN FEATS OF A PIONEER FATHER AND MOTHER

DIED WITH THEIR BOOTS ON—THE MESSACAR FAMILY

14.

Spring, May 15, 1814

Spring sowing completed, fields green with promise,
mills running day and night, men gone to battle,
women and children alone, long night of terror,
sun dawns on hearts, filled with foreboding,

hanging white flags, tokens pacific.
Beautiful village and mill, shining in morning,
just past noon a smoking ruin.

Colonel Campbell the burner of Dover, but leading the Americans,
a local turncoat, Captain Markle; carnage universal,
a private from Gordon's company fires his musket,
breaks the forelegs of a fine English cow.

A party of sailors mans the artillery, kills hogs in the streets,
severs limbs, heads and shoulders left to rot.
After the conflagration, one home standing,

stands still today, monument to a lady, kindly
Mrs. McQueen gifts the soldiers fresh bread and milk
for the burners of Dover.

15.

Epilogue, at attention, please

Brave pioneers, old pioneers, brave old pioneers,
erecting cabins, heaping logs
damning Black Creek
bridging the River Lynn
building the Mill
in Glorious Old Norfolk

SILENCE

CHILDREN AT THE BEACH

Take thy bliss, O Man!
And sweet shall be thy taste & sweet thy infant joys renew!

William Blake, *Visions of the Daughters of Albion*

1.

Where the water tower stands
St Andrew street like a comma
curls back to Main.

2.

Remember mottled wet beach like this after the rain?
No, but I remember morning beach when the rays were small.

3.

When you came here with your family
and you were twelve and you were starting to look
and starting to get together and tell your jokes
and a couple was behind the high school
and a policeman finds you and you says you're only necking
and he says, well, put your neck back in your pants
and get outta here.

4.

You can get smashed by this lake,
but I don't know what this means.

5.

Diamond flashing water coming into shore
before a large white yacht.

6.

Days when through the cloud
a narrow band of sun lights.

7.

Farm kids from Hagersville
with their six foot inflatables—
the big kings of the surf.

8.

Remembering: days when there is just one blanket
after another—the whole beach a quilt.

Seeing a fishing boat with gulls
behind a yellow paper bag
floating like a large berg on the horizon:
a double sail.

9.

Norfolk Hotel
Ladies and Escorts
presenting Mr Bruise B.

Mr Bruise B,
loves like a bee
kisses like a wasp,
oh no
Mr Bruce B.

oooooh eeeee—Mr Brian R.
mouth like a bar
when he does he goes up far
ooo-----eeee

oooo--eeeeee
oo-ah ah
ting tang
wally wally bing bang
oo--eeee--oooo--aa--aa--
ting tang tanga
wallywally bing bang

Stevie Crozier—here he is
waiting for his hard on to go down to piss
while pencilling on the wall seven foot tall
Polonius Sucks

John and Mary up in a tree
K.I.S.S.I.N.G.
first comes love
then comes marriage
then comes Mary
with a baby carriage
oh-oh

Tiny Tim
went to the doctor
doctor wasn't in
went to the nurse
nurse had the curse
oh oh Tiny Tim

10.

The Dover Rose comes in loaded. On the ground is a mass of orange net, and green and white and grey buoys. The drawbridge rises. For a second, a bird is caught in the shutter of the rising bridge. A paper flies back, a moment of a newspaper article on falling through the ice. You don't see any change in the fish around here, so far, some one says to us. We take off our sandals, they're no good for climbing in the sand; we avoid stepping on the cigarette butts with our bare feet. The bell goes again. My new perm is getting stiff with sand. The bell rings again and the bridge begins to rise; it is hot. A small blue sailboat cuts the water. Followed by a coral yacht. It continues to be hot. Three kids, two bikes, and three fishing poles pass us as we climb.

Brian and Tony climb up to the top of Bank street, on the edge of the highway. A yellow forklift passes. We head for a path of dead thistles, snap, snap, down the path toward the children, Dougie and Shelley. She is 13, he is 14. We buy them each a foot long hot dog, and then a strawberry ice cream cone. Only ten cents for a full scoop.

The limits are my voice, statistics crowding out the voices of the past, The Cat People, The Scots, The Irish, The English. The map offers the mileage, the population of each hamlet, the distance to the Rural Life Mission, to the Hagersville Florist, to St Andrew's Church. I can hear those Europeans in the names of places, honouring early voyagers, Selkirk Provincial Park, the hamlet of Jarvis, Nottingham, Goville, Hatorp, homesickness memorialized in sound.

I'm the International Harvester, gathering in the crops, manning the Lift Bridge, wandering the main street, measuring up the past. Here's Mr Vary, of 421 Main street, 87 years old; he had a store in 1908, when Dover's population was 1500. He tells me it's taken 60 years to double; he's going to hold on now 'til he's a hundred. Have something to report then.

11.

The contours of spirit are pasted on the windows of the GOSPEL MISSION, faded red and white paper mums visible on a table inside, a lattice exhorting passersby:

Repent ye and believe the gospel. Mark 1:15

Repent ye therefore and be converted, that your sins may be blotted out. Acts 3:19

The wages of sin is death but the gift of God is eternal life through Jesus Christ our Lord. Romans 6:23

Our Lord, how excellent My Salvation, My Glory, My Strength, My Refuge. Greetings the Scotts Brazil. Psalms 8:1 and Psalms 62-67.

The Prayers of Christ: Our Father who Art in Heaven. Matt 6:9-13

Father forgive them, for they know not what they do: Luke 23:34

For I have given unto them the words which thou gavest me. John 17:8-10

The Bible says Taste and See that the Lord is Good. Psalms 8:8

Jesus saves. Acts 16:31

12.

Coming upon
The Blue Pickerel :
Fishburgers / Good Food
The Best Fish in Town
Try Some For The Halibut

13.

Because this is what it's like. Port Dover is a hot summer's day, eating Arbors and walking on the boardwalk.

Canal Street, Canal Street
The Street that I adore
God Damn son of a bitch
I couldn't find a whore

ARCADE Barrage
R-U- Truly Mated
Frigit Naughty
Sex Less
Sex I
Deposit 10 cents

Drag the Net
what da you get—smelt
Gill with the net
ain't dead yet: perch

14.

Let Joseph rejoice with the Turbot,
whose capture makes the poor fisher-man sing.
Christopher Smart, *Jubilate Agno*

15.

She looks sharp without the camera, says Dougie.
Through it, she doesn't even look smart.

16.

You guys are lucky, says Dougie.
I don't learn nothing in school.
The other kids are too noisy.
No, she's not young, but she's not old either.
She's got veins in her hands.

V
THE NARRATIVE OF JOHN SIMPLE

May I by myself sing a true song,
Speak of my travels, how I suffered in days of hardship

Anonymous, *The Seafarer* (*Exeter Book*, 8th or 9th century)

1.

Decoratin' the Commercial or the Norfolk, oh yes, I've done my decoratin' in my time. Fishins like farmin, fishins in the stone-age. We employ a lot of men, 700 in the factory alone. I dont mind fishin cheap if the folks gets it cheap. We get 4 cents a pound for fish, folks pay 89 cents a pound. Now there's too much middle work there. Oh yes, folks is always settin around here late drinkin coffee. They was all alcoholics, they got big hearts. There was my uncle now, in Ghosport. Has the biggest heart, would give you anything, and shot his wife, my aunt, and his little girl, and then himself. And that was all due to drink. You gotta watch it. Ghosports like the Ozarks, and the people there all drink, but they—we—all got big hearts. You'd think the government would subsidize us.

And now my neighbours all say to me, Johnny, sell your house. Sell your house now it's all paid for. Sell it and buy a nice house for you and the wife, now you're not getting any younger, and what, well what do I need a house for. We're happy here, and I know I figure I got three years left at it. But when I see the younger men tired out before me, and me taking the wheel all the time, why sometimes we get in here at ten at night, and we leave here again at two in the morning, trying to cut out some time on the road to Burwell, and I says Officer, wasn't no call for me to be snotty to him, if you done somethin wrong, you done somethin wrong. Yes, you says, my speedometer cables broke, so if you says so, well, okay, you're right, and if we can save a little time we do, so you just go on and write out that ticket, cause we got work to do tonight The FISH IS RUNNIN...

2.

...you should have seen his hands. Do you know Rolley's Brown Salve? Why, it's the best thing, and his hands, poor John's hands, all swollen from the fish line, and now good as new. Yes, all over—that's right.

Now ain't that so, ain't that just like you. Now she loves animals. Well. I like em myself, and that there one cost $125. We call it Minny, and what a commotion the night the coon died. Never got a lick of sleep that night.

Sometimes I feel like I'm losing all respect for the law. Now laws is laws.
('No John, laws okay.') Now laws is laws, but when I see that woman and her little child up there in the country, while he's in jail, and them maybe with nothing to eat, well, then I gets a bit disgusted.

3.

Let Crippus rejoice with Leviathin—God be gracious to the Soul of Hobbes, who was no atheist, but a servant of Christ and died in the Lord— I wronged him God forgive me....As earth increases by Behemoth, so the sea likewise enlarges.

Christopher Smart, *Jubilate Agno*

Muriel Cooper, only woman fisherwoman on the lake.
Fishes in an open boat. Hauls in by hand.

Yes, there's one lady fisherman in the lake, and she and her husband used to together. But they has a big parting, and now she goes it alone. And one day we was out, and there was quite a blow, and someone says to me, he must be crazy out here in a little open boat like that. And I says, that's no man, that's a lady, and he says you're lyin, and I says you just know, and sure enough, there she was.

4.

Well I helps as many as I kin, doin what ya kin, and plays square and you dont want fer nothing like a house. I puts it all into the boats and, well, I like a nice car, I got that there over in Simcoe, and I give the Galaxy to the boy, 'cause he needs all his money for his drinking, and well...

5.

Let Nicanor rejoice with the Skeat—Blessed be the name of the Lord Jesus in fish and in Shew-bread,
which ought to be continually on the altar,
now more than ever, and the want of it is the Abomination of Desolation
spoken of by Daniel.
Christopher Smart, Jubilate Agno

I shows them the statement each week, and the wife figures out the percentages, and then if she's made a mistake, well they can see it to fix it. There's some who just tells em what they make, and have made a new house out of their men—do you call that right now?

And I got caught in a gale up near Goderich, and sunk her, and it cost me $8000 to lift her up. Then I was wiped out, and she says where ya goin? And I says to get me a tug. And she says, Where at Woolco? (I had but a quarter in my pocket.) And I says, just a tug, and when I come back, she says, Well did you get it? And I says, Yep I got it. Got me one, and worked on it day and night. And pretty soon I had her in the water, all open you know. Hauling the nets in by myself, and pretty soon fishing was bad for others, and they started to say how lucky I was. Now, do you call that luck—one man in an open boat?

Well, one day I came in and found the dock is just plastered with them.
I'd been gone two days. Got blowed clean out.
Well I says ya didn't want me then, so how come ya wants me now?
Now I'm not having none of it.

6.

Oh, we fished out of Burwell and Stanley, and I'm from near Brighton. I made as sweet a little deal on the Alma as a man could wish for. And he says, get your wife to read it over, and think about it. And I says no thinking needed. And he says I'd like your wife to read it, and I says, that was three years ago, get out your pen, with some ink in it, she don't do fishing, besides anything I do is alright with her.

Now is that fair...an imaginary line, and me not even allowed to go to court to say what's right, and what I did, because the licence wasn't in my name, and now the Alma settin' there and two or three hundred dollars a day gone, and people with families to feed, now is that right, how's a man to feed his family if he can't work, and the government not givin' a subsidy.

      Sometimes you just think the law must be wrong.

7.

...Newton is ignorant for if a man consult not the WORD how should he understand the WORK ?

Christopher Smart, *Jubilate Agno*

Gill netting in an open tug / two days hauling in the perch / go to bed at 11 / and get up and leave at 2 / going on 4 years now on the Alma.

Four Atlantic Interludes from Tantramar and Grand Pré with Charles G.D. Roberts and Bliss Carman (1886, 1893)

8.

Pale with scurf of the salt
seamed and baked in the sun
pile of rope and block
beaded net wound round the reel
dripping and dark from the sea.

9.

Salt, raw scent at the marge
men at the windlass groan
reel and net are coiled—
then each man home.

10.

Do the far off seas pale
by these fluttering slopes of peas?

11.

Glory falls with the sun,
may it abide
the coming of the tide.

12.

From the wide prairies, in deep struggling sea,
In rolling breakers, bursting to the sky
In tumbling surfs, all yellow'd faintly thro
With the low sun—in mad conflicting crests
Voic'd with low thunder from the hairy throats
Of the mist-buried herds and for a man
To stand amid the cloudy roll and moil
The phantom waters breaking overhead.
Shades of vex'd billows bursting on his breast
Torn caves of mist walls with sudden gold
Resealed as swift as seen—broad shaggy fronts
Fire-ey'd and tossing on impatient horns
The wave impalpable—was but to think
A dream of phantoms held him as he stood....

Isabella Valancy Crawford, *Malcolm's Katie* (1884)

13.

I hate a lie. There's no call to lie. If a man says to me, it's for beer, I says okay, no call to lie, you understand. We've had our trouble, she and I, but I knew it was getting nowhere.

Well no, he's living down there in that shanty. And he scrubs it, two or three times a week, and he is always busy. And he has a pile of fruit on the tablecloth, wouldn't just eat off a chrome table. A pile of bananas, they eat a lot of fruit, you know. He's so careful, if he has a cigarette, he's got ashtrays all over, and is always mending the nets. Gerimias Atilia—that's his name, we calls him Gerry. They eat a lotta fruit, you know, and there's no call to live like an animal, he don't.

I don't know about spending a pile of money to tell us what fish is running. When they tell us what size nets to take out, and that the perch is all done, and we take out little nets, and we catch little perch alright—8 or 9 and a half inches. Now does that seem right to spend that pile of money?

It's a big lake. Sometimes they're down, sometimes near the top.
Near the bottom, they're growing. How can anybody know the run then?

14.

People are wonderful, you know we get around, and they're just wonderful, all heart. Well, we've got to make allowances for the times we're living in.
Can you imagine one of those early settlers coming here now, can you imagine what he'd think of this?

15.

Oh, yes. I was looking for that paper to show you. It was, I think, thirty years ago, Bee here's got a scrapbook full of the history of this place. Her father was the one that built that bridge, when he was eighty or ninety years old. And he invented a smelt machine for cleaning them. Then, too, at eighty-seven, he made this engine which runs all day on only a teaspoon of gas; it runs all day on the fumes. Got no education, of course, but he's mighty smart without any learning. You'd think a man's mind would just have dried up, now wouldn't you?

16.

I try to give them a chance. No one else will, and just married.
And with a drinking problem, I says, you be sober for the morning, and he wasn't. But I let him try, lots of people wouldn't.

17.

Donny lets the net unfurl;
he lets the net unfurl;
the net unfurls.

VI
ARRIVALS

1.

Rain on the River

In the fog we drift hither and yon over the dark waves.
At last under a maple, our little boat finds shelter.

Above the veil of mist, from time to time, there lifts a sail.

2.

Coming in

We rowed ashore. Early this morning we took a tour along the coast of the bay.
It's all a montage now, looking back on it.
You are in my mind here, Sarah, your presence.
Two white birds in a windy sky.

3.

the sixteenth

...what is it? The dream began it. The writing started then.
Any point to this is there, blowing all through it, invisible, yet heard.
I am afraid to say like the wind in the trees.

4.

the seventeenth

Tonight the dream came again, and a healer touched me with his index finger,
just below my clavicle, saying pain is serpentine—here is its point of entry—here is its
point of exit. As he touched me all the pain of my life came rushing out,
and you were there, watching, as it left.

That's all for now.
Adios.
Until we see each other again, carry my love with you,
B

*What can with the great Leviathan compare,
Who takes his pastime in the mighty main?
What, like the Sun, shines thro' the realms of air,
and gilds and glorifies th' ethereal plain—
Yet what are these to man, who bears the sway;
For all was made for him—to serve and to obey.*

Christopher Smart, *Hymn To The Supreme Being
on Recovering from A Dangerous Fit of Illness
(1756)*

AFTERWORD AND ACKNOWLEDGEMENTS

In all my encounters with the great bodies of water of the globe I have enjoyed the companionship of those who share my passion for our seas and oceans and lakes: Brian Ramer, Nick Youngman, and Armando Pajalich. But I want especially to acknowledge Brent Whipple who has given me permission to quote from, redact and recast those original letters whose shape inspired 'The Sailor's Letter' section of my book. His own book "Tattoo" is forthcoming.

I suspect everyone who writes from Ontario's deep southwest has been led and lessoned by the writings of James Reaney. As an editor, he nourished several generations; as a writer, he inspired us all with the magic of our legends and folk heroes.

'The Early Settlement' materials are based on *Papers and Records of the Ontario Historical Society*, the *Norfolk Historical Society*, as well as *Historical Highlights of Norfolk County*, and *The Burning of Dover by* Dr John A. Bannister (1965). Sketches of pioneer life and place names for the area are vividly presented in E.A. Owen's *Pioneer Sketches of Long Point Settlement, or Norfolk's Foundation Builders and Their Family Genealogies* (1898), as well as *Norfolk Place Names* by Henry Smith Johnson (1959).

A version of the 'Children at the Beach' section of *Fishing Poems* was published decades ago by bill bissett at his blue ointment press.

One stage of the development of this manuscript was supported in 2000 by a Writers' Reserve Grant from The Ontario Arts Council.

As always, I am grateful to the City of Toronto and its nourishing of the arts through Toronto Artscape. Many of my books have been grown in watery tranquility on the Toronto Islands at Toronto Artscape, Gibraltar Point.

As I was preparing the final version of these *Fishing Poems* for production, I went to a concert, organized by the St Andrew's Society of Toronto, at the El Mocambo. The El Mo, as it is affectionately known, has been a famous rock and roll bar for decades and those of a certain age might recall the Rolling Stones concert there which has lived on in Canadian iconography as the sure sign of the end of the marriage of our then Prime Minister Pierre Elliott Trudeau and his lovely wife Margaret Sinclair.

It was June 21, 2014, when I went to the El Mo to this celebration of Celtic Culture. The large upstairs space was festooned in the blue and white flags of St Andrew of Scotland and with few exceptions all the men present wore kilts, even the ticket taker was in a skirt, although his was made of denim. There was a full pipe band, bass drums, and a small troop of highland dancers, and one of the groups playing was my friend Rory Sinclair's trio, with Rory on the pipes, Stephanie on fiddle and Gaye on guitar. Caledon County not only played old Celtic standards, but also, with a little help from their friends, updated, or predated, songs with bagpipes, like Chuck Berry's 1964 stand-out *You Never Can Tell (Teenage Wedding)*, a song which I first heard Chuck Berry himself perform at the Rock 2 ten hour concert at the Summer Garden in Port Dover on September 5 in 1971.

The occasion for the celebration that June 2014 evening at the El Mo was not the centenary of World War I, but the Battle of Bannockburn, where the Scots defeated the English army under Edward II. This battle occurred on June 24, 1314. Seven hundred years might have passed for some, but I realized on that humid and windy summer night, on Spadina Avenue in Toronto, that my child's sense of the past in the present was not an isolated moment confined to the rural Ontario of fifty years ago but is continuous with our plummeting toward the future.

ROCK 2

TEN HOURS SUN

sunday sept 5
2pm – midnite

SWIM FUN

CHUCK BERRY
POWERHOUSE
Black Sheep
RHINOCEROUS

woolies

rumour

Summer Garden
PORT DOVER

ADVANCE SALE $2.75
AT DOOR 3.25

available at
all hiway boutiques   alec sherman's   summer garden